the STORY of the WORLD

Volume 1: Ancient Times

From the Earliest Nomads to the Last Roman Emperor

TESTS AND ANSWER KEY

25th Anniversary Expanded Edition

WELL-TRAINED MIND PRESS

Charles City, Virginia

www.welltrainedmind.com

Photocopying and Distribution Policy

Publisher's Cataloging-in-Publication
(Provided by Cassidy Cataloguing Services, Inc.)

Title: Test book and answer key : Story of the world. Vol. 1, Ancient times.
Other titles: Story of the world. Vol. 1, Ancient times : test book and answer key
Description: 25th anniversary expanded edition. | Charles City, Virginia : Well-Trained Mind Press, [2026] | Series: Bauer, Susan Wise. Story of the world.
Identifiers: ISBN: 9781944481889 (paperback)
Subjects: LCSH: World history--Examinations, questions, etc. | Civilization--Examinations, questions, etc. | History, Ancient--Examinations, questions, etc. | Nomads--History--Examinations, questions, etc. | LCGFT: Examinations. | BISAC: EDUCATION / Home Schooling. | EDUCATION / Schools / Levels / Elementary. | EDUCATION / Teaching / Subjects / Arts & Humanities.
Classification: LCC: D20 .B35 2026 | DDC: 909--dc23

How to Use These Tests and Answer Key

These Tests and their accompanying Answer Key are designed to go along with Susan Wise Bauer's *The Story of the World, Volume 1: 25th Anniversary Expanded Edition*. These tests are designed for those teachers and parents who want to evaluate their students' understanding of the major ideas and dates found within *The Story of the World, Volume 1* text. After your student reads each chapter of the book, he should be given time to review the reading before taking that chapter's test. If you are using *The Story of the World, Volume 1 Volume 1: 25th Anniversary Expanded Edition Instructor Guide*, you should go through the chapter's Read & Review Questions, Narration Exercises, Map Work activities, and other complementary projects and readings. These will reinforce and expand your student's knowledge of the material. For more information on the *Volume 1 Instructor Guide* and accompanying *Student Workbook*, please visit welltrainedmind.com.

Although *The Story of the World, Volume 1* is intended for students between grades 1 and 6, we recommend that these tests be used with students in grade 4 and up. They can be used with younger students, but you might find that the Read & Review questions in the *Instructor Guide* are sufficient for evaluating your student's comprehension. For more ideas, support, and suggestions, visit the *Well-Trained Mind* message boards, at welltrainedmind.com/forums.

the STORY of the WORLD

Volume 1: Ancient Times

TESTS AND ANSWER KEY

25th Anniversary Expanded Edition

Name ______________________________ Date __________

The Story of the World, Vol. 1

Chapter 1 Test: The Earliest People

A. Fill in the blanks.

1. A ____________________ is a person who wanders or roams around.
2. In warm places, the first families lived in ____________________.
3. In colder, rocky places, they lived in ____________________.
4. One of the best places for the earliest people to live was ________________.
5. Early farmers would dig ____________________ to bring water from the river to their fields.

B. Multiple Choice. Circle the letter of the best choice.

6. When the nomads had eaten most of the food in one place they would __________.
   a. plant more food
   b. move to another place
   c. send a few people out to look for more
   d. start a war
7. What kind of food did women and children help provide for the family?
   a. large animals such as deer and bison
   b. vegetables
   c. berries, nuts, roots, and lizards
   d. bread
8. What kind of food did men provide for the family?
   a. honey and eggs
   b. vegetables
   c. berries, nuts, and roots
   d. large animals such as deer and bison

9. Nomads built tents using _________ and wooden frames.
    a. animal hides
    b. mud bricks
    c. rocks
    d. reeds and grasses
10. The first farmers grew ___________.
    a. olives and figs
    b. apple trees
    c. grain
    d. berries and nuts
11. Early farmers used a machine called a shaduf to ___________.
    a. harvest their grain
    b. water their crops
    c. plant seeds
    d. till the soil
12. Farmers began to build _________ so that they could help each other water and tend their crops.
    a. stone walls
    b. villages
    c. canals
    d. houses

C. True or False. Write the word "true" or "false."

_________ 13. The Fertile Crescent was a good place to live because there was water, good soil, and plenty of grass and plants.

_________ 14. The early farmers moved from place to place like nomads.

_________ 15. Farmers began to build their houses out of mud bricks and reeds.

_________ 16. Early farmers began to raise cattle and pigs.

_________ 17. Villages began to build stone walls around their villages to keep their animals inside the village.

_________ 18. Jericho was one of the earliest cities.

Name ____ Date ______________

The Story of the World, Vol. 1

Chapter 2 Test: Egyptians Lived on the Nile River

A. Fill in the blanks.

1. The Nile River is on the continent of ____________________.
2. Every year the Nile River would ____________________.
3. The people who lived in the Nile delta were called the ____________________.
4. The people who lived along the straight part of the Nile River were called the

   ____________________.
5. The king of Egypt became known as the ____________________.

B. Multiple Choice. Circle the letter of the best choice.

6. What is the Nile Delta?
   a. the area at the top of the river where it splits into several different little rivers
   b. the name of the mountain range near the Nile River
   c. the part of the river that dried up each year
7. Why did the Egyptian farmers like to see the river flood?
   a. It would give them more drinking water.
   b. It would make the air cooler.
   c. It would bring up rich dirt that was good for the plants.
   d. It would make it easier to fish.
8. How many tribes lived along the Nile during Egypt's early history?
   a. one
   b. two
   c. three
   d. four

9. When the Egyptians were united, what did the king wear to show that he ruled the entire country?
    a. a red crown
    b. a shepherd's crook
    c. a double crown with a white spike at the center and a red band on the outside
    d. a gold crown

10. According to one Egyptian myth, Set tricked his brother, Osiris, into lying down in a ________.
    a. river
    b. field
    c. bed
    d. coffin

11. What happened to Osiris after he lay down?
    a. Set threw him into the river.
    b. Ra helped him climb out.
    c. He was buried.
    d. He cried until he had no tears left.

12. What happened after Osiris came back to life?
    a. Isis wrapped him in linen so that he became the first mummy.
    b. The Nile filled back up and overflowed.
    c. Set built a beautiful coffin for him.
    d. The Nile wept over his death and ran dry.

C. True or False. Write the word "true" or "false."

__________ 13. When the White Crown King and the Red Crown King fought for control of Egypt, the White Crown King won.

__________ 14. The Egyptians worshipped many gods.

__________ 15. Osiris was the god of the sun and the chief god.

__________ 16. The Egyptian pharaoh was worshipped as a god.

__________ 17. Egyptian farmers would build their houses very close to the river.

__________ 18. Egyptian stories about the gods often tried to explain why the Nile overflowed each year.

Name ____________________________________ Date ____________

The Story of the World, Vol. 1

Chapter 3 Test: The First Writing

A. Fill in the blanks.

1. The ___________________ were among the earliest people to use writing.
2. They wrote with pictures called ___________________.
3. The people who lived in ___________________ found a better way to write using wet clay.
4. They wrote with pictures called ___________________.

B. Multiple Choice. Circle the letter of the best choice.

5. The Egyptians carved their pictures into _________.
    a. stone tablets
    b. wet clay
    c. sand
    d. paper
6. Where is Mesopotamia?
    a. in Egypt
    b. below the Nile River
    c. between the Tigris and Euphrates Rivers
    d. next to Egypt
7. What did the Sumerians do with their tablets after they carved them?
    a. get them wet to harden them
    b. bake them until they were hard
    c. roll them up into scrolls
    d. fold them up
8. The Egyptians learned to make a special kind of paper called _________.
    a. meso
    b. cuneiform
    c. hieroglyphics
    d. papyrus

9. What is something that is not good about this special paper?

   a. It starts to fall apart over time.

   b. It is easier to write on paper than on clay or stone.

   c. It can be folded or rolled up into a scroll.

   d. It takes up less room.

10. We do not know a great deal about what happened in Egypt after they started writing on __________ because these writings have crumbled and disappeared.

   a. stone

   b. wet clay

   c. paper

C. True or False. Write the word "true" or "false."

__________ 11. The stone tablets carved by the Egyptians lasted for a long time and they were quick to make.

__________ 12. Writing in clay was harder than carving in stone.

__________ 13. The word Mesopotamia means "between two rivers."

__________ 14. Egyptian paper was made from reeds that grew along the banks of the Nile.

__________ 15. We know a lot about early Egyptian and Sumerian history because of the writings that have been found.

Name ____ Date ______________

The Story of the World, Vol. 1

Chapter 4 Test: The Old Kingdom of Egypt

A. Fill in the blanks.

1. During the Old Kingdom of Egypt, the Egyptians began to make _________________ for the first time.
2. Only _________________ were allowed to embalm bodies.
3. The Egyptians believed that the _________________ would be weighed on a special pair of scales when a person reached the afterworld.
4. A mummy was put into _________________ different coffins before it was buried.
5. Pharaohs were buried in _________________ to keep their treasures safe.

B. Multiple Choice. Circle the letter of the best choice.

6. How long did it take to make a mummy?
   - a. several days
   - b. over two months
   - c. two weeks
   - d. one year
7. What did the priests do with most of the organs inside a dead body?
   - a. They were covered in special spices and placed in canopic jars.
   - b. They were covered in special spices and placed back in the body.
   - c. They were wrapped in linen strips.
   - d. They were covered with gold.
8. What was placed between the strips of linen wrapped around a mummy?
   - a. salt
   - b. spices
   - c. wine
   - d. pieces of jewelry

9. A ___________ was put onto the mummy's face so that the gods would recognize him.
    a. sarcophagus
    b. gold mask
    c. beautiful painting
    d. papyrus

10. What were the pyramids made out of?
    a. stone
    b. clay
    c. gold
    d. wood

11. How did the Egyptians build the pyramids?
    a. They used elephants to drag the blocks.
    b. They built ramps and used ropes.
    c. They used cranes and bulldozers.
    d. They carved the pyramids out of mountains.

C. True or False. Write the word "true" or "false."

__________ 12. The Egyptians believed it was important to embalm a body so that the dead could enter the afterworld.

__________ 13. The burial chamber would be filled with everything that a dead person would need in the afterlife such as furniture, food, clothes, games, and jewelry.

__________ 14. A sarcophagus was a big stone coffin inside the burial chamber.

__________ 15. Once a tomb was sealed it was never again opened or disturbed by robbers.

__________ 16. The Great Sphinx is an imaginary animal with the body of a man and the head of a lion.

Name ____ Date _____________

The Story of the World, Vol. 1

Chapter 5 Test: The First Sumerian Dictator

A. Fill in the blanks.

1. ____________________________________ is the area of land between the Tigris and Euphrates rivers.
2. The _________________________ lived in this area.
3. The cities in Sumer were called _____________________ because each city was like a separate country with its own king and army.
4. A man named _________________ wanted to make all of the cities into one country.
5. He grew up in the city of ___________________.

B. Multiple Choice. Circle the letter of the best choice.

6. What did the villages in Sumer build to protect themselves?
   a. fences
   b. clay tablets
   c. castles
   d. thick walls with high towers
7. Sargon became the _________ in the king's palace.
   a. cook
   b. cup-bearer
   c. soldier
   d. general
8. Sargon became so popular that he convinced the _________ to follow him.
   a. army
   b. king
   c. farmers
   d. queen

9. How did Sargon unite all of the cities in Mesopotamia?
    a. He poisoned all of the other kings.
    b. He became very popular with all of the people.
    c. He fought over fifty wars.

10. Sargon named his new empire __________.
    a. Sargonia
    b. Sumer
    c. Akkadia
    d. Mesopotamia

C. True or False. Write the word "true" or "false."

__________ 11. One story about Sargon says that he was found floating down the Euphrates River in a basket when he was a baby.

__________ 12. Sargon convinced the army to kill the king.

__________ 13. All of the cities in Mesopotamia were glad that Sargon was their new king.

__________ 14. Sargon sent soldiers to every conquered city to make sure the people were following his laws.

__________ 15. A military dictatorship is when a ruler uses his army to make sure people obey him.

Name ______________________________________ Date ____________

The Story of the World, Vol. 1

Chapter 6 Test: The Jewish People

A. Fill in the blanks.

1. Abram lived in one of the cities in Sargon's empire called ________________.
2. The Bible tells the story of Abram in the book of ________________.
3. God told Abram to move to the land of ________________.
4. Abraham's grandson, Jacob, had ________________ sons.
5. Jacob's son, Joseph, became a powerful leader in ________________.

B. Multiple Choice. Circle the letter of the best choice.

6. Abram's father, Terah, was worried that _______.
    a. other cities or the Gutian tribes might attack Ur and he would lose all of his riches
    b. he did not have enough money
    c. the moon-god would not protect him
    d. Abraham did not have a son to carry on the family business
7. Terah moved his family, including Abram and Sarai, to _______.
    a. Babylon
    b. Egypt
    c. Haran
    d. Canaan
8. When Abraham was older than your grandparents, he had a son named _______.
    a. Benjamin
    b. Judah
    c. Jacob
    d. Isaac

9. What special gift did Jacob give to Joseph?
    a. a beautiful coat
    b. a flock of sheep
    c. his own servant
    d. a shepherd's crook

10. What did Joseph's brothers do to him?
    a. They killed him.
    b. They sold him to traders as a slave.
    c. They threw him in a pit and left him there.
    d. They made fun of him.

11. The pharaoh of Egypt had a dream about ________.
    a. vines and grapes
    b. bread baskets and birds
    c. the sun, moon, and stars
    d. seven fat cows and seven skinny cows

12. What did Pharaoh do after Joseph told him what his dream meant?
    a. He killed Joseph.
    b. He sent Joseph back to Canaan.
    c. He made Joseph second in command in Egypt.
    d. He gave Joseph to Potiphar.

C. True or False. Write the word "true" or "false."

__________ 13. Abraham means "father of many children."

__________ 14. There were ten tribes that became known as the nation of Israel, or the Jewish people.

__________ 15. God promised to bless Abraham if Abraham would worship only God.

__________ 16. Joseph's brothers were jealous of the special gift that Jacob gave to Joseph.

__________ 17. When Joseph's brothers came to Egypt to buy food during the famine, they recognized Joseph immediately.

__________ 18. When the Israelites moved to Egypt, they began to worship the same gods that the Egyptians worshipped.

Name ____ Date ____________

The Story of the World, Vol. 1

Chapter 7 Test: Hammurabi and the Babylonians

A. Fill in the blanks.

1. Hammurabi ruled the whole southern part of Mesopotamia called _______________.
2. He wrote down a set of laws called ___________________________.
3. The Babylonians called the time that it took the earth to go all the way around the sun once _______________.
4. They divided this time period into ______________ months.

B. Multiple Choice. Circle the letter of the best choice.

5. Hammurabi wanted his empire to be governed by _________.
   a. just laws
   b. a strong army
   c. religious priests
   d. a powerful king
6. Who had to obey Hammurabi's laws?
   a. only men
   b. everyone but the king
   c. everyone
   d. only soldiers
7. Where did Hammurabi write down his laws?
   a. They were written on a scroll in a ziggurat.
   b. They were written on clay tablets.
   c. They were carved on the walls of the palace.
   d. They were carved on a stone monument.

8. Hammurabi encouraged his people to learn more about __________.

    a. the gods
    b. the laws of other cities
    c. farming
    d. nature

9. People in Babylon believed that they could find out what the gods were doing by __________.

    a. praying and offering sacrifices
    b. watching the movements of the planets and stars
    c. asking the priests
    d. observing nature

C. True or False. Write the word "true" or "false."

__________ 10. The people of Mesopotamia lived with war all the time because the citystates were constantly fighting with each other.

__________ 11. Hammurabi believed that the chief god of Babylon, Marduk, made him king so that he could become rich.

__________ 12. Hammurabi wanted people to follow his laws because they were right—not because soldiers were making them obey.

__________ 13. The Babylonians could tell the difference between stars and planets.

__________ 14. The Babylonians divided an hour into 50 minutes.

Name ______________________________________ Date ____________

The Story of the World, Vol. 1

Chapter 8 Test: The Assyrians

A. Fill in the blanks.

1. Shamshi-Adad ruled the ____________________ part of Mesopotamia.
2. The name of his empire was the ____________________ Empire.
3. The story of ______________________ is one of the oldest fairy-tales in the world.
4. According to this story, a ____________________ ate a magic plant that made it live forever.

B. Multiple Choice. Circle the letter of the best choice.

5. Where did Shamshi-Adad live?
   a. Babylon
   b. Assur
   c. Kish
   d. Egypt
6. Shamshi-Adad wanted to _______.
   a. be a fair ruler
   b. rule the whole world
   c. become a priest
   d. be a noble king
7. How did Shamshi get people to obey him?
   a. He killed anyone who would not do exactly what he said.
   b. He rewarded the people who obeyed him.
   c. He had fair laws.
   d. He promised to let the people choose their own leaders.
8. What did the people in Mesopotamia think of the Assyrians?
   a. They thought the Assyrians were fair rulers.
   b. They did not think that the Assyrians were good warriors.
   c. They thought the Assyrians had good laws.
   d. They were scared of the Assyrians.

9. What happened after Shamshi-Adad died?
    a. His two sons ruled together peacefully.
    b. Gilgamesh became the new ruler.
    c. Hammurabi conquered the Assyrians.
    d. His two sons split his empire.

10. According the story of Gilgamesh, what did the sky god, Anu, send to help the people?
    a. a monster named Enkidu
    b. a new king
    c. a man named Utnapishtim
    d. a strong army

C. True or False. Write the word "true" or "false."

__________ 11. Shamshi-Adad ruled by fear and cruelty.

__________ 12. Hammurabi was not as cruel as Shamshi-Adad.

__________ 13. Gilgamesh was a good king, and his people loved him.

__________ 14. Gilgamesh and Enkidu eventually became good friends.

__________ 15. According to the story, Gilgamesh ate a magic plant that made him live forever.

Name ____ Date ______________

The Story of the World, Vol. 1

Chapter 9 Test: The First Cities of India

A. Fill in the blanks.

1. Ancient people began to make money by ____________________ with other cities.
2. Many ancient cities were built near ____________________.
3. The people of India built cities near the ____________________ River.
4. Their cities were often built around huge circular mounds called ________________.

B. Multiple Choice. Circle the letter of the best choice.

5. Ancient cities often used rivers as a road because ________.
   a. the people could not agree where to build roads
   b. it was safer than building roads
   c. it was easier and faster to travel by boat than across land
   d. the people did not have enough money to build roads
6. Farmers in India grew grain like the Mesopotamians, but they also grew ________.
   a. corn and melons
   b. rice and beans
   c. cotton and melons
   d. corn and rice
7. Another way that the Indian farmer was different from the Mesopotamian farmer was that he used ________.
   a. elephants and water buffalo
   b. boats to trade his crops
   c. iron tools
   d. canals to irrigate

8. Why were the cities in the Indus Valley built around citadels?
    a. to make it easier for the farmers to work together
    b. to protect the people in case enemies attacked
    c. to make transportation easier
    d. to help the people become rich
9. What were the houses in the Indus Valley made of?
    a. stone
    b. cedar logs
    c. animal skins
    d. mud bricks baked hard in ovens
10. One ancient story passed down in India tells of a hunter and a flock of __________.
    a. quail
    b. elephants
    c. water buffalo
    d. chickens

C. True or False. Write the word "true" or "false."

__________ 11. The people of India found that it was easier to travel over the mountains than to travel by sea.

__________ 12. The people of ancient India built comfortable houses with courtyards, wells, and even toilets and drains.

__________ 13. For hundreds of years, no one knew that the great cities of India ever existed because they had been deserted and covered with dirt and sand.

__________ 14. The cities of India were eventually united into one large kingdom.

__________ 15. No one knows for sure what happened to the citadel cities of India.

Name ________________________________ Date ____________

The Story of the World, Vol. 1

Chapter 10 Test: The Far East: Ancient China

A. Fill in the blanks.

1. The people of China first lived between the ________________ River and the Yangtze River.
2. In China, farmers grew crops, especially ________________, because it grows well in wet ground.
3. The Empress Lei Zu discovered a way to make the fabric called ________________.
4. A ________________ is when a family rules one country for many years.
5. The Chinese used a special kind of writing called ________________.

B. Multiple Choice. Circle the letter of the best choice.

6. Why was China called the "Far East"?
   a. The Chinese people had to travel far to the east to trade with other people.
   b. It was all the way the way to the edge of the world to the Mesopotamians.
   c. It was far away from the Yangtze River.
   d. The Yangtze River was east of China.
7. How did Lei Zu discover the new kind of fabric?
   a. She had a dream about it.
   b. Her servant girl told her how to make it.
   c. A cocoon fell into her cup of tea.
   d. She saw some cocoons in a tree and thought they would make pretty fabric.
8. Why don't we know many facts about the first great leader of China?
   a. Many of the written records say different things.
   b. He lived a very long time ago, and there are no written records about his empire.
   c. There are no stories or legends about him.
   d. No one understands Chinese writing.

9. During the rule of the Shang family, the Chinese began to use __________.
   a. bronze
   b. gold
   c. silver
   d. iron

10. The Shang family also used a kind of writing in which words look like __________.
    a. straight lines
    b. wavy lines
    c. letters
    d. pictures

11. What kind of animals did farmers in China raise?
    a. sheep and goats
    b. elephants and water buffalo
    c. turkeys and geese
    d. pigs, chickens, and cows

12. What kind of soil did the Chinese farmers need to raise their special kind of grain?
    a. very wet soil
    b. very dry soil
    c. soil that is wet part of the year and dry part of the year
    d. rocky soil

C. True or False. Write the word "true" or "false."

__________ 13. Huang Di was the first great leader of China who united the many small villages into one empire.

__________ 14. The Shang dynasty ruled for about 500 years.

__________ 15. The mulberry plant was an important plant in Ancient China.

__________ 16. In the story about Chin, it was the mother's duty to make sure that the father had everything that he needed in the morning.

__________ 17. Chin's job helping his father in the fields was very easy.

Name ____ Date _____________

The Story of the World, Vol. 1

Chapter 11 Test: Ancient Africa

A. Fill in the blanks.

1. The _________________ is a large, dry, and hot area west of Egypt.
2. The only water in this area is found in _________________, little patches of land where water collects and a few scrubby palm trees can grow.
3. This area in Africa was not always dry; it was once a green, fertile place full of trees and _________________.
4. _________________ is a favorite character of African storytellers.

B. Multiple Choice. Circle the letter of the best choice.

5. Why don't we know much about ancient Africa?
   a. The people of Africa didn't leave written records or thousands of artifacts.
   b. Many of the written records say different things.
   c. We have no stories or legends from Africa.
   d. No one understands African writing.
6. What did archeologists find when they dug down through the hard dirt of the Sahara?
   a. clay tablets with writing on them
   b. bronze weapons
   c. thousands and thousands of artifacts
   d. pollen from trees and seeds from grasses and flowers that do not grow in the Sahara today
7. What happened in the Sahara?
   a. The rains got scarcer and the grass and trees dried up.
   b. Too much rain flooded it.
   c. Many of the tribes of people who lived there fought wars and killed each other.
   d. The Egyptians conquered the tribes of people.

8. Where did the people who once lived in the Sahara move?
    a. east to Egypt
    b. south to the center of Africa
    c. east to Mesopotamia
    d. north to the coast of the Mediterranean Sea

9. Which word best describes Anansi?
    a. honest
    b. tricky
    c. brave
    d. fearful

10. What kinds of food did Anansi find in the different villages?
    a. peanuts, lettuce, and rice
    b. wheat and corn
    c. rice and melons
    d. yams, plantains, and rice

C. True or False. Write the word "true" or "false."

__________ 11. The people who once lived in the Sahara were farmers, just like those who lived in the Fertile Crescent.

__________ 12. Archeologists have found paintings on the walls of caves that show how Africans once lived.

__________ 13. Yams are like sweet potatoes.

__________ 14. Plantains are a special kind of rice.

__________ 15. The people of Africa passed many stories down from person to person.

Name ______________________________ Date __________

The Story of the World, Vol. 1

Chapter 12 Test: Life in Early Crete

A. Fill in the blanks.

1. The ____________________ lived on an island called Crete.
2. Crete is a long, skinny island in the ____________________________ Sea.
3. The people of Crete used to entertain themselves by leaping over ____________________.
4. The people of Crete had the first ______________________, an army that fights on water.
5. The ____________________ was a monster who was half man and half bull.

B. Multiple Choice. Circle the letter of the best choice.

6. The people of Crete held their leaping festivals to honor __________.
   - a. the king
   - b. their gods
   - c. their children
   - d. nature
7. Why was it so dangerous to travel on the sea in ancient times?
   - a. The weather made the water rough and choppy.
   - b. There were no maps so the people did not know where to sail.
   - c. Pirates controlled the sea.
   - d. The people did not know how to make boats.
8. King __________ was a legendary king of Crete.
   - a. Nebuchadnezzar
   - b. Minos
   - c. Aegeus
   - d. Ariadne

9. This king fed _________ to the monster that lived in the maze beneath his palace.
    a. girls and boys from a nearby city
    b. his slaves
    c. bulls
    d. his daughters

10. Theseus was the prince of the nearby city, ______.
    a. Egypt
    b. Nineveh
    c. Knossos
    d. Athens

11. What did Theseus use to find his way through the maze so he could kill the monster?
    a. a map
    b. a mirror
    c. a ball of wool
    d. a sword

12. When Theseus was sailing home, his father ______.
    a. jumped off a cliff
    b. ran to the shore to meet him
    c. planned a huge celebration to welcome him home
    d. was killed by one of his enemies

13. Many historians believe the people left Crete because ______.
    a. a hurricane forced them to leave
    b. they were tired of living on an island
    c. a volcano erupted nearby
    d. pirates captured them

C. True or False. Write the word "true" or "false."

__________ 14. The children who participated in the leaping festivals had a safe job.

__________ 15. These children were given beautiful clothes, jewelry, and gold.

__________ 16. Ariadne helped Theseus kill the monster.

__________ 17. The Aegean Sea was named after the father of Ariadne.

__________ 18. The island of Thera sank into the sea.

Name ______________________________ Date ____________

The Story of the World, Vol. 1

Chapter 13 Test: The Middle Kingdom of Egypt

A. Fill in the blanks.

1. When Amenemhet became pharaoh, he wanted to make Egypt larger, so he decided to conquer the country to the south of Egypt called ________________.
2. The Egyptians renamed this country ________________.
3. Amenemhet's family ruled Egypt for many years and became a powerful ________________.
4. Nomads from ________________ called the Hyksos conquered Egypt after Amenemhet's family ruled.

B. Multiple Choice. Circle the letter of the best choice.

5. What happened to the Old Kingdom of Egypt?
   - a. It grew much larger when the people conquered the land of Canaan.
   - b. It grew more powerful.
   - c. It became weak and powerless.
   - d. It was conquered by the Nubians.
6. Amenemhet's reign was the beginning of the __________.
   - a. Middle Kingdom of Egypt
   - b. Old Kingdom of Egypt
   - c. New Kingdom of Egypt
   - d. Second Kingdom of Egypt
7. Amenemhet knew there was __________ in the hills and ground of the country to the south of Egypt.
   - a. bronze
   - b. silver
   - c. ivory
   - d. gold

8. When the people to the south of Egypt were conquered by the Egyptians, they ______.
    a. became Egyptian
    b. moved to Canaan
    c. rebelled against the Egyptians
    d. moved to the Sahara

9. After Amenemhet's family ruled, Egypt once again became ______.
    a. stronger and more powerful
    b. weak and powerless
    c. larger
    d. richer

10. The Egyptians thought that the Hyksos were ______.
    a. good rulers
    b. rude, unclean, and uncivilized
    c. prosperous and wealthy
    d. polite and good-looking

11. Who drove the Hyksos out of Egypt?
    a. Amenemhet
    b. the Egyptian priests
    c. a group of Egyptian princes
    d. the Canaanites

C. True or False. Write the word "true" or "false."

__________ 12. Egypt became stronger even when there were bad pharaohs.

__________ 13. One woman from the conquered country to the south became the queen of Egypt.

__________ 14. The Hyksos used the same kind of weapons that the Egyptians used.

__________ 15. The Hyksos called the Egyptians "shepherd kings."

__________ 16. Using the weapons of the Hyksos, the Egyptians became one of the most powerful kingdoms in the whole world.

Name ________________________________ Date ____________

The Story of the World, Vol. 1

Chapter 14 Test: The New Kingdom of Egypt

A. Matching. Match each pharaoh with the correct description.

____ 1. Hatshepsut

____ 2. Amenhotep

____ 3. Thutmose

____ 4. Tutankhamen

a. fought both the Nubians and the Hyksos and made Egypt twice as big

b. became pharaoh even though she was a woman; wore men's clothes and a false beard

c. was only seven when he became king; was buried with many treasures that were not found until three thousand years later

d. wanted the Egyptians to worship just one god

B. True or False. Write the word "true" or "false."

__________ 5. Before he became pharaoh, Thutmose was a general in the Egyptian army.

__________ 6. Most Egyptians worshipped only one god.

__________ 7. Polytheism is the worship of just one god.

__________ 8. When Tut's tomb was discovered, many items had already been stolen.

__________ 9. After it was discovered, people said that there was a curse on Tut's tomb.

C. Multiple Choice. Circle the letter of the best choice.

10. The New Kingdom of Egypt is sometimes called the ______.
    a. Middle Kingdom of Egypt
    b. Second Kingdom of Egypt
    c. Last Kingdom of Egypt
    d. Golden Age of Egypt

11. How did Thutmose become the pharaoh of Egypt?
    a. He married the pharaoh's daughter.
    b. He killed the old pharaoh.
    c. He persuaded the army to crown him as king.
    d. The priests named him as the new pharaoh.

12. Thutmose did not try to conquer Babylon because _________.

    a. He knew Babylon was too powerful to conquer.

    b. Babylon was too far away.

    c. His army did not want to cross the Euphrates River.

    d. He thought that Babylon did not have enough gold or riches.

13. Which of the following were Egyptian women not allowed to do?

    a. get married and have children

    b. serve at the temple

    c. rule as pharaoh

    d. become dancers

14. As pharaoh, Hatshepsut _________.

    a. fought many wars

    b. brought back gold, incense, monkeys, and elephants from Africa

    c. worshipped only one god

    d. ruled for only four years

15. A monotheist is someone who _________.

    a. worships many gods

    b. worships only one god

    c. worships no gods

    d. does not believe in any gods

16. When Amenhotep died, the Egyptian people _________.

    a. buried him with all of his treasures

    b. built many monuments to him

    c. worshipped only one god

    d. tried to forget he had ever been pharaoh

17. The Valley of the Kings is a place in Egypt where _________.

    a. many of the pharaohs lived

    b. the pyramids are located

    c. many of the pharaohs were buried

    d. archaeologists have found old temples

Name ______________________________ Date ____________

The Story of the World, Vol. 1

Chapter 15 Test: The Israelites Leave Egypt

A. Fill in the blanks.

1. The Israelites are descended from ____________________.
2. The Egyptians made the Israelites their ____________________.
3. ____________________ was an Israelite who grew up in the palace of the pharaoh.
4. When the Israelites left Egypt, God parted the waters of the ____________________.
5. The story of the Israelites leaving Egypt is found in the Bible in the book of ____________________.

B. Multiple Choice. Circle the letter of the best choice.

6. The Israelites were unusual in the ancient world because ____________.
   a. they were monotheists
   b. they were polytheists
   c. they were very rich
   d. they had very small families
7. Why did the Israelites move to Egypt?
   a. They were trying to escape from the Babylonians.
   b. They wanted to conquer the Egyptians.
   c. They were looking for gold.
   d. There was a famine in Canaan where they lived.
8. The Egyptians started to worry that the Israelites might ____________.
   a. try to steal all of their gold
   b. decide to move back to Canaan
   c. attack the Egyptians and take their kingdom away
   d. start worshipping the Egyptian gods

9. What did the pharaoh decide to do about the Israelites when they had more and more children?
    a. make the Israelites worship the Egyptian gods
    b. send the Israelites back to Canaan
    c. kill every Israelite baby boy
    d. send the Israelites to the Sahara Desert

10. Who found a baby floating in a basket on the Nile?
    a. pharaoh's daughter
    b. pharaoh
    c. Miriam
    d. a servant girl

11. God sent __________ plagues on Egypt to show that he was more powerful than the gods of Egypt.
    a. five
    b. ten
    c. eight
    d. six

12. Where did the Israelites go when they left Egypt?
    a. to the coast of the Mediterranean Sea
    b. to the Sahara Desert
    c. to Mesopotamia
    d. back toward Canaan

C. True or False. Write the word "true" or "false."

__________ 13. While they lived in Egypt, the Israelites worshipped only one God.

__________ 14. The Israelite nation grew smaller and smaller in Egypt.

__________ 15. Moses was born into an Egyptian family and was raised in the palace.

__________ 16. When the Israelites asked to leave Egypt, pharaoh said yes.

__________ 17. When the Israelites left Egypt, the Egyptians chased them, but were drowned.

__________ 18. The Israelites later became a powerful kingdom in their own right.

Name ____ Date ______________

The Story of the World, Vol. 1

Chapter 16 Test: The Early Greeks

A. Matching. Match each group of people with the correct description.

____	1. Mycenaeans	a.	also called the Sea people; they conquered the Greeks
____	2. Dorians	b.	invaded Greece from the North
____	3. Philistines	c.	Greek people who conquered the island of Crete
____	4. Minoans	d.	lived on the island of Crete

B. Multiple Choice. Circle the letter of the best choice.

5. The Mycenaeans built ____________ all around the Aegean Sea.
   a. colonies
   b. palaces
   c. walls
   d. temples

6. The Mycenaeans were good fighters because they made their weapons and armor from ____________.
   a. bronze
   b. wood
   c. gold
   d. iron

7. The Mycenaeans were the first Greeks to use ____________ in battle.
   a. javelins
   b. swords
   c. horses
   d. bows and arrows

8. How did the Mycenaeans live?
   a. The wandered around from place to place.
   b. They lived in houses made of stone or wood.
   c. They lived in caves.
   d. They built tents with sticks and animal hides.

9. How were the barbarians different from the Mycenaeans?
    a. The barbarians had regular jobs.
    b. The barbarians lived in better houses.
    c. The barbarians couldn't read or write.
    d. The barbarians were great craftsmen.

10. The barbarians had ___________ weapons.
    a. wooden
    b. gold
    c. bronze
    d. iron

11. The barbarians used ___________ to kill Greek chariot drivers from a long distance away.
    a. swords
    b. javelins
    c. horses
    d. cannons

12. The time period after the Greeks were conquered is called the _______________.
    a. Dark Ages
    b. Golden Age
    c. Mycenaean Era
    d. Missing Time Era

C. True or False. Write the word "true" or "false."

__________ 13. The Mycenaeans learned how to build ships from the Minoans.

__________ 14. The Mycenaeans were the first great Greek civilization.

__________ 15. The barbarians thought the Greeks were ignorant, smelly and uncivilized.

__________ 16. We know much about the barbarians who conquered the Greeks because they left many written records.

Name ____ Date _____________

The Story of the World, Vol. 1

Chapter 17 Test: The Phoenicians

A. Fill in the blanks.

1. The Phoenicians were the group of people living in ______________________.
2. The Phoenicians sailed all around the ____________________________________.
3. Two important Phoenician cities were ____________________ and _______________.
4. The Phoenicians were famous for making ____________________ and ____________________.

B. Multiple Choice. Circle the letter of the best choice.

5. Which of these sentences is not true about the area where the Phoenicians lived?
   a. It was rocky, sandy, and dry.
   b. It wasn't a good place to raise animals because there wasn't enough grass or water.
   c. It was surrounded by steep craggy hills.
   d. It was easy to get into and out of.
6. What did the Phoenicians use to make glass?
   a. snails
   b. sand and lye
   c. rocks
   d. cedar logs
7. What was the color of the Phoenicians' famous dye?
   a. green
   b. blue
   c. purple
   d. gold
8. The Phoenicians used ___________ to make their special dye.
   a. flowers
   b. lye
   c. snails
   d. cedar logs

9. The color of this dye was often called "the color of kings" because ___________.
    a. the dye was so expensive
    b. only kings were allowed to wear it
    c. it was the Phoenician king's favorite color
    d. the dye smelled so good when it was being made

10. The Phoenicians started _______________, little settlements of people, in many of the places where their ships landed.
    a. states
    b. city-states
    c. colonies
    d. countries

C. True or False. Write the word "true" or "false."

__________ 11. When the Israelites walked from Egypt back up to Canaan, they were moving into an empty country.

__________ 12. The northern part of Canaan wasn't a very good place to grow wheat.

__________ 13. The Phoenicians were the first glassmakers to invent glass blowing.

__________ 14. According to the story, Dido left her home because she was afraid of her husband.

__________ 15. Dido wanted to build her city near the water so that ships would visit and trade with her.

Name ____ Date _____________

The Story of the World, Vol. 1

Chapter 18 Test: The Return of Assyria

A. Fill in the blanks.

1. The Assyrian army used shields made out of _________________.
2. Ashurbanipal was _________________ to the cities he conquered.
3. He lived in the city of _________________.
4. He was the first _________________.

B. Multiple Choice. Circle the letter of the best choice.

5. Which of these countries did the Assyrians not conquer?
   a. Babylon
   b. Egypt
   c. India
   d. Canaan
6. What did Ashurbanipal like to do for fun?
   a. write poetry
   b. hunt lions with bows and arrows
   c. make glass
   d. listen to music
7. The Assyrians were almost impossible to beat because they _________.
   a. fought in pairs
   b. used bronze swords
   c. dug tunnels under the ground
   d. wore so much armor
8. What did most of the people in the Assyrian Empire think about Ashurbanipal?
   a. They hated him.
   b. They thought he was a fair ruler.
   c. They admired him.
   d. They were happy to obey him.

9. What did Ashurbanipal do so that people would remember him?
    a. He held a grand parade.
    b. He told many stories.
    c. He built a beautiful temple.
    d. He collected many books.
10. During Ashurbanipal's time, books were made out of __________.
    a. paper
    b. stone
    c. clay
    d. scrolls

C. True or False. Write the word "true" or "false."

__________ 11. To defeat the Babylonians, the Assyrians dug canals and flooded the city.

__________ 12. The Assyrians conquered the Israelites and never allowed them to return to Canaan.

__________ 13. To capture a city, Assyrian soldiers would dig tunnels under the city walls.

__________ 14. Ashurbanipal built beautiful gardens with strange plants from far away.

__________ 15. Ashurbanipal created the first hospital in the world.

Name ______________________________ Date ______________

The Story of the World, Vol. 1

Chapter 19 Test: Greece Gets Civilized Again

A. Matching. Match each person with the correct description.

____ 1. Poseidon

____ 2. Cyclops

____ 3. Homer

____ 4. Odysseus

a. a Greek poet who wrote down some of the old Greek stories

b. a Greek warrior who fought in the Trojan War

c. a giant with only one eye in the center of his forehead

d. the Greek god of the sea

B. Multiple Choice. Circle the letter of the best choice.

5. What happened to the barbarians who invaded Greece?

   a. They moved back to their original lands.

   b. They were eventually defeated by the Mycenaeans.

   c. They became civilized and learned to live like the Greeks.

   d. The were killed when a volcano erupted.

6. What kind of crops did the Greeks learn to grow?

   a. olives, grapes, and figs

   b. corn and beans

   c. oranges and cotton

   d. yams and bananas

7. For fun, the Greeks liked to ______________.

   a. dance

   b. attack their neighbors

   c. sing

   d. draw pictures

8. We know more about the early Greeks than we know about the barbarians because they wrote things down using their own ______________.

   a. pens

   b. alphabet

   c. pictograms

   d. cuneiforms

9. According to tradition, Homer __________.

   a. did not know how to write.

   b. was deaf.

   c. could not walk.

   d. was blind.

10. One famous Greek story tells about a war when the Greeks attacked the city of __________.

    a. Knossos

    b. Troy

    c. Mycenae

    d. Nineveh

11. The Greeks held ______________ to honor Zeus and to celebrate courage and strength.

    a. the Olympic Games

    b. the Trojan Games

    c. chariot races

    d. yearly wars

12. The pentathlon was an athletic event in which the athlete had to compete in _______ different events.

    a. ten

    b. four

    c. five

    d. seven

C. True or False. Write the word “true” or “false.”

_________ 13. Many of the letters we use today are borrowed from the ancient Greeks.

_________ 14. The Phoenicians had one of the first alphabets.

_________ 15. The *Iliad* is a poem about a Greek soldier trying to sail back home.

_________ 16. To escape from the giant’s cave, the Greek soldiers held on to the bellies of the giant’s sheep.

_________ 17. Both men and women were allowed to compete in the Olympic Games.

_________ 18. The Olympic Games were held every six years.

Name ______________________________ Date ____________

The Story of the World, Vol. 1

Chapter 20 Test: Sparta and Athens

A. Fill in the blanks.

1. The people of ________________ wanted their children to be wise and educated.
2. The people of ________________ wanted their children to be strong and brave.
3. When the citizens of Athens needed to vote about something, they would gather at a special meeting place called the ________________.
4. A ________________ is when people vote on the laws and the leaders.

B. Multiple Choice. Circle the letter of the best choice.

5. The Greeks were different from the Persians because all of the Greeks _________.
   a. didn't speak the same language
   b. didn't obey the same king
   c. didn't dress the same
   d. didn't worship the same gods
6. Sparta was ruled by _________ kings.
   a. many
   b. elected
   c. warrior
   d. educated
7. Spartan boys were never allowed to _________.
   a. complain
   b. run
   c. eat
   d. exercise
8. When Spartan boys were 20 years old, they had to _________.
   a. get married
   b. leave the army
   c. vote
   d. pass a test of fitness and bravery

9. What were girls in Sparta supposed to do?
    a. have children who would fight for Sparta
    b. learn to read and write
    c. join the army with the men
    d. learn to take care of the household

10. Which of these things did the people of Athens not vote on?
    a. their leaders
    b. the gods they would worship
    c. their taxes
    d. whether they should go to war

11. The Athenians thought it was important to be educated so that __________.
    a. people could read
    b. citizens could understand how to vote properly
    c. people would have better jobs
    d. boys would know how to fight

12. ____________ was a famous Greek who said ignorant people will always obey tyrants.
    a. Cyrus
    b. Sparta
    c. Athens
    d. Plato

13. What were all girls in Athens supposed to do?
    a. have children who would fight for Athens
    b. learn to read and write
    c. learn how to vote
    d. learn to take care of the household

C. True or False. Write the word "true" or "false."

__________ 14. Sparta and Athens were very similar cities.

__________ 15. All men in Sparta were allowed to vote.

__________ 16. Boys in Athens learned reading, writing, mathematics, music, and poetry.

__________ 17. Girls in Athens learned how to sew, raise a garden, and take care of children.

__________ 18. The people of Athens wanted to be ruled by tyrants.

Name ______________________________ Date ____________

The Story of the World, Vol. 1

Chapter 21 Test: The Greek Gods

A. Matching. Match each person with the correct description.

____	1. Zeus	a.	the king of the Greeks
____	2. Hera	b.	the king of the gods
____	3. Aphrodite	c.	the wife of Menelaus
____	4. Athena	d.	the prince of Troy
____	5. Paris	e.	the goddess of love and beauty
____	6. Helen	f.	the wife of Zeus
____	7. Menelaus	g.	the goddess of strife
____	8. Eris	h.	the goddess of war

B. Multiple Choice. Circle the letter of the best choice.

9. The Greeks were ____________, which means they worshipped many gods.
   - a. polyglots
   - b. Confucians
   - c. polytheists
   - d. monotheists

10. The Greeks believed that their gods lived on __________, the highest mountain in Greece.
    - a. Mount Olympus
    - b. Mount Zion
    - c. Mount Ararat
    - d. Mount Sinai

11. Why did Zeus want to start a war on earth?
    - a. He was bored.
    - b. The goddess of war needed something to do.
    - c. He liked having wars.
    - d. He thought there were too many people on the earth.

12. What did Zeus make that caused a war?

    a. a golden crown

    b. a golden orange

    c. a crown of olive leaves

    d. a golden apple

13. _______________ was asked to judge who was the most beautiful.

    a. Poseidon

    b. Paris

    c. Menelaus

    d. Eris

14. Why did he choose Aphrodite as the most beautiful?

    a. He wanted to be king of the whole world.

    b. He wanted to win every battle he fought.

    c. He wanted to have the most beautiful woman on earth.

    d. He wanted to obey Zeus.

15. What happened when Helen fell in love with Paris?

    a. The Trojan War began.

    b. Paris killed Menelaus.

    c. Hera killed Helen.

    d. Helen and Paris got married.

C. True or False. Write the word "true" or "false."

__________ 16. The Greeks believed that the gods were very interested in what men were doing.

__________ 17. The Greek gods were always kind and helpful to men.

__________ 18. The Trojan War lasted for many years.

Name ________________________________ Date ____________

The Story of the World, Vol. 1

Chapter 22 Test: The Rise of Rome

A. Fill in the blanks.

1. Rome was founded on top of ______________________ hills.
2. Rome is located in the country of ______________________.
3. The most important Italian tribe was called the ______________________.
4. Their kings wore special robes called ______________________, with purple borders to show everyone how important the king was.

B. Multiple Choice. Circle the letter of the best choice.

5. According to the legend, who were Romulus and Remus?
   - a. the first two Etruscan kings
   - b. two brothers who founded Rome
   - c. the first two consuls of Rome
   - d. two of the Roman gods
6. Romulus and Remus were raised by __________.
   - a. a wolf and then a shepherd
   - b. their grandfather
   - c. the servant who was told to drown them
   - d. the king of Rome
7. Why did Romulus kill Remus?
   - a. He was angry because Remus wanted to be king.
   - b. He was jealous of Remus because their grandfather liked him better.
   - c. He was angry because Remus jumped over his wall.
   - d. He was tired of sharing everything with him.
8. The Etruscans traded with the ____________.
   - a. Phoenicians
   - b. Egyptians
   - c. Romans
   - d. Greeks

9. Which of the following did the Romans not learn from the Etruscans?
    a. how to dress
    b. painting and music
    c. about the Greek gods
    d. how to fight

10. A ________________ is a symbol of power that shows a bundle of rods with an ax blade.
    a. fasces
    b. consul
    c. dime
    d. patrician

11. Who could vote on laws and leaders in Rome?
    a. all men who weren't slaves
    b. only the rich and powerful men
    c. all of the men
    d. only the consuls

12. How many consuls were appointed in Rome?
    a. one
    b. ten
    c. five
    d. two

C. True or False. Write the word "true" or "false."

_________ 13. The Roman Empire lasted for hundreds and hundreds of years.

_________ 14. Ancient people liked stories about their kings that made them seem like great fairy-tale heroes.

_________ 15. Rome was a democracy just like Greece.

Name ______________________________________ Date ____________

The Story of the World, Vol. 1

Chapter 23 Test: Babylon Takes Over Again!

A. Fill in the blanks.

1. Babylon had a powerful king who went mad and lived like a wild ________________.
2. This story is recorded in the Bible in the book of ________________.
3. The king of Babylon was worried about ________________, a country to the east.
4. This king also built the ________________________________ of Babylon for his wife. They are one of the Seven Wonders of the Ancient World.

B. Multiple Choice. Circle the letter of the best choice.

5. What was the name of the great king of Babylon?
   a. Nebuchadnezzar
   b. Ashurbanipal
   c. Marduk
   d. Ishtar
6. Which country was never conquered by the Babylonians?
   a. Assyria
   b. Canaan
   c. Egypt
7. What did the Babylonians do to the city of Nineveh?
   a. They made it their new capital.
   b. They destroyed it.
   c. They left it alone.
   d. They flooded it.
8. The king of Babylon built a famous _________ to honor the chief goddess, Ishtar.
   a. gate
   b. garden
   c. library
   d. temple

9. The king of Babylon went mad because ___________.

    a. his wife was so sad
    b. he was weary from fighting so many wars
    c. he was so worried about other nations attacking him
    d. he thought he was greater than everyone, including God

10. Who did the king of Babylon marry?

    a. the queen of Egypt
    b. the princess of the country to the east
    c. an Israelite princess
    d. a princess from Assyria

11. What did she miss the most about her old home?

    a. her palace
    b. the flat land
    c. the mountains and gardens
    d. her family

C. True or False. Write the word "true" or "false."

__________ 12. The Babylonians forgave the Assyrians for destroying Babylon.

__________ 13. The Babylonian Empire was not as large as the Assyrian Empire.

__________ 14. After the king of Babylon lost his mind, he never got better.

__________ 15. The king of Babylon married his wife because he thought she was the most beautiful woman he had ever seen.

__________ 16. The new queen of Babylon was homesick.

Name ______________________________________ Date ____________

The Story of the World, Vol. 1

Chapter 24 Test: The Medes and the Persians

A. Fill in the blanks.

1. The Babylonians and the ____________________ finally defeated the Assyrians.
2. The Persians were a tribe of ______________________ who lived at the edge of Media.
3. ________________ became a great king of Persia.
4. This king became the greatest king in the world at that time, but there was still one country that he had not conquered. This country was ________________.

B. Multiple Choice. Circle the letter of the best choice.

5. What did King Astyges of Persia do with his grandson?
    a. He ordered his chief advisor to kill him.
    b. He gave him many gifts of gold and jewels.
    c. He taught him how to be a great king.
    d. He trained him to be a shepherd.
6. Harpagus disobeyed his master by ___________.
    a. not worshipping the king's gods
    b. letting the king's grandson run away
    c. not punishing the Persians when they did not follow the king's laws
    d. ordering a shepherd to kill the baby instead of doing it himself
7. _________ helped Cyrus become king.
    a. Astyges
    b. Croesus
    c. Harpagus
    d. Shamshi-Adad
8. The Persians thought Cyrus was a great warrior and a _________ king.
    a. selfish
    b. lazy
    c. cruel
    d. good and fair

9. Croesus had more ___________ than anyone in the world.

    a. gold
    b. land
    c. palaces
    d. soldiers

10. Cyrus was able to easily conquer Babylon because _____________.

    a. the Babylonian Empire was not very strong.
    b. the city did not have a wall around it.
    c. the Babylonians hated their king.
    d. he had many more soldiers than the Babylonian king.

11. When Cyrus became king of Babylon, he allowed the Jews to ___________.

    a. have important positions in his government
    b. return to Palestine
    c. build their own temple in Persia
    d. elect their own king

12. The Jews called Cyrus ___________.

    a. a cruel tyrant
    b. the Anointed of the Lord
    c. the King with the Golden Touch
    d. the shepherd king

C. True or False. Write the word "true" or "false."

__________ 13. The Assyrians and the Babylonians fought each other for many years, and the rulers of the world kept changing.

__________ 14. The Medes and the Babylonians also fought against each other.

__________ 15. Astyges was worried by a dream he had.

__________ 16. Cyrus was raised as a shepherd on a mountain.

__________ 17. When Cyrus grew up, he was smaller than all the other boys his age.

__________ 18. Cyrus conquered land from Egypt all the way to India.

Name ____ Date ______________

The Story of the World, Vol. 1

Chapter 25 Test: The Aryans of India

A. Fill in the blanks.

1. The Aryans were a group of people who came to India from ________________________.
2. The Aryans settled near two rivers, the Indus River and the ____________________ River.
3. The religion of these people was called ____________________.
4. In this religion, people belong to one of four groups called a ____________________.

B. Multiple Choice. Circle the letter of the best choice.

5. What kinds of crops did the Indian farmers raise?
    a. wheat and rice
    b. melons and wheat
    c. corn and beans
    d. cotton and rice
6. Every year the sacred river in India would ___________.
    a. dry up
    b. overflow
    c. change direction
    d. grow longer
7. Who did the people of ancient India believe had given them their river?
    a. Siddhartha
    b. Rig Veda
    c. Ganga
    d. Shiva
8. Which group of people was the most important?
    a. farmers and traders
    b. noble warriors
    c. brahmin or priests
    d. untouchables

9. How did people know which group they belonged to?
    a. They were born into it.
    b. They married into it.
    c. They were assigned a group at school.
    d. They were assigned a group by the king.
10. What were the people called who didn't belong to any group?
    a. farmers and traders
    b. noble warriors
    c. brahmin or priests
    d. untouchables
11. Why did Siddhartha leave his palace?
    a. He was bored.
    b. He wanted to see what was outside the palace walls.
    c. He thought that a god was calling him to go.
    d. He wanted to help people.
12. Siddhartha became known as ____________.
    a. Shiva
    b. Ganga
    c. Buddha
    d. Purusha

C. True or False. Write the word "true" or "false."

__________ 13. The people of ancient India raised horses and cows.

__________ 14. The job of the Untouchables was to protect the priests from enemies and to rule India.

__________ 15. In India, you could only marry someone who belonged to the same group as you.

__________ 16. Siddhartha taught that people could find happiness by leading a good life.

__________ 17. Today, no one follows the teachings of Siddhartha.

Name ______________________________________ Date ____________

The Story of the World, Vol. 1

Chapter 26 Test: Writing, Fighting, and Thinking in China

A. Fill in the blanks.

1. Chinese writing changed from *pictograms* (pictures that looked like the things they represented) into writing that looked less like the words they stood for. This writing is called __________________.
2. In this later form of writing, each word is called a __________________.
3. Writers in ancient China first used special sharp paintbrushes made out of ____________________.
4. The Chinese were the first people to use ___________________, a process of pressing characters into books with ink and blocks of wood.

B. Multiple Choice. Circle the letter of the best choice.

5. Confucius lived around the same time as ____________.
   a. Narmer
   b. Buddha
   c. Abraham
   d. Qin Zheng
6. Like Buddha, Confucius taught that people could learn to be _________ even if they were poor.
   a. wealthy
   b. smart
   c. happy
   d. sad
7. Confucius hated ___________, which was happening all around him.
   a. war and turmoil
   b. wealth
   c. peace
   d. wastefulness

8. He taught that people should __________ authority.
    a. respect
    b. rebel against
    c. ignore
    d. disobey
9. He also taught that people in authority should be __________ to those who are beneath them.
    a. kind
    b. cruel
    c. just
    d. hateful
10. The sayings of Confucius were collected together into a book called ______________.
    a. *The Sayings of Confucius*
    b. *The Writings of Confucius*
    c. *The Wisdom of Confucius*
    d. *The Analects of Confucius*

C. True or False.

_________ 11. Do not do unto others, what you would not want others to do to you.

_________ 12. It is the wiser person who takes rather than gives.

_________ 13. The followers of Confucius tried to band together to stop the Warring States from fighting.

_________ 14. The followers of Confucius focused on controlling their own behavior.

Name ______________________________ Date ____________

The Story of the World, Vol. 1

Chapter 27 Test: The Wars of the Greeks

A. Fill in the blanks.

1. Sparta and ____________________ were always fighting with each other.
2. These two cities decided to become friends and allies when ____________________ tried to invade Greece.
3. The ____________________ was a temple built in honor of Athena, the goddess of war.
4. ____________________ won the Peloponnesian War.

B. Multiple Choice. Circle the letter of the best choice.

5. The war with Persia lasted for _________.
   - a. twenty years
   - b. six weeks
   - c. two months
   - d. twenty-five years
6. Who was outnumbered at the Battle of Marathon?
   - a. Sparta
   - b. Salamis
   - c. Persia
   - d. Athens
7. After the Battle of Marathon, a messenger ran all the way to __________ to deliver the news of victory.
   - a. Sparta
   - b. Salamis
   - c. Athens
   - d. Persia
8. According to legend, what happened to the messenger?
   - a. He became a hero.
   - b. He died of exhaustion.
   - c. He was made the new king.

9. When Greece was at peace they became famous for their ______.
    a. architecture
    b. food
    c. paintings
    d. books
10. What caused the Peloponnesian War?
    a. Sparta and Athens were afraid that another country would try to invade them again.
    b. The Greeks could not agree on the best kind of government.
    c. Sparta and Athens were afraid that the other city would become too powerful.
    d. Each Greek city wanted to have the most beautiful buildings and statues.
11. What happened in the city of Athens while Sparta was attacking them?
    a. The Persians joined with the Spartans.
    b. A plague broke out inside the city walls.
    c. The people began to starve to death.
    d. They ran out of water.
12. What did Alcibiades do that helped end the war?
    a. He convinced the Athenians to surrender.
    b. He became a traitor and showed the Spartans how to defeat the Athenians.
    c. He killed the Spartan king.
    d. He killed the greatest Athenian general.

C. True or False. Write the word "true" or "false."

__________ 13. When the Persian king sent a messenger to Greece, the Greeks threw the messenger down a well.

__________ 14. During one battle, the Athenians refused to come help the Spartans because they were having a religious festival.

__________ 15. After the Battle of Marathon, Persia finally stopped attacking Greece.

__________ 16. A frieze is a picture carved in marble.

__________ 17. The people in Greek friezes look very real.

Name ______________________________ Date ____________

The Story of the World, Vol. 1

Chapter 28 Test: Alexander the Great

A. Fill in the blanks.

1. Philip was the king of ____________________.
2. King Philip wanted to take over the ____________________ Empire, but he died before he could attack.
3. The Pharos was a giant ____________________.
4. Alexander built a great city named ____________________ in Egypt.

B. Multiple Choice. Circle the letter of the best choice.

5. The name "Alexander" means "protector of __________."
   a. the world
   b. the sky
   c. men
   d. all people
6. Bucephalus was the name of Alexander's __________.
   a. father
   b. mother
   c. horse
   d. dog
7. What did Alexander do to the Gordian Knot?
   a. He cut it in half.
   b. He untied it.
   c. He burned it.
   d. He asked the gods to help him solve it.
8. Why was Alexander unable to conquer all of India?
   a. He did not know how to use elephants in battle.
   b. The Indian soldiers far outnumbered Alexander's soldiers.
   c. He died before he got to India.
   d. His soldiers refused to fight.

9. What did Alexander do so that people of the future would remember him?
    a. He built a huge library.
    b. He built many cities.
    c. He wrote many books.
    d. He had many statues made of himself.

10. How did Alexander die?
    a. His soldiers killed him.
    b. He caught the plague.
    c. He died of old age.
    d. No one knows for sure; he just became weaker and weaker.

11. After Alexander died, his generals divided his empire into ____________ parts.
    a. two
    b. five
    c. three
    d. four

C. True or False. Write the word "true" or "false."

__________ 12. Egypt was the first area conquered by King Philip.

__________ 13. Alexander tamed his horse by turning him so he couldn't see his shadow.

__________ 14. Alexander was only 20 years old when he became king.

__________ 15. Ptolemy I became the new pharaoh of Egypt after the death of Alexander.

__________ 16. After Alexander died, his generals got along well together.

Name ______________________________ Date __________

The Story of the World, Vol. 1

Chapter 29 Test: The Mauryan Empire of India

A. Fill in the blanks.

1. Cities in the ancient world were stronger if they were ____________________ together with other cities.
2. ____________________ was a famous ruler of the Mauryan Empire.
3. He followed the religious teachings of ____________________.
4. Some of the best-known writings from the Mahayana Tripitaka are called the ______________________________.

B. Multiple Choice. Circle the letter of the best choice.

5. Why did the Indian kings want to unite the many different cities?
   - a. They wanted India to be a strong, unified country.
   - b. They wanted to be able to attack other countries.
   - c. They needed to help each other with farming.
   - d. They wanted to be like their neighbors.
6. Why did Asoka not want to fight with an army?
   - a. He did not have enough money to pay his soldiers.
   - b. He did not think he could trust an army.
   - c. He wanted to defeat everyone by himself.
   - d. He saw the suffering that his soldiers had caused.
7. Asoka made laws against __________.
   - a. eating meat
   - b. having hospitals
   - c. being cruel to animals
   - d. dishonesty

8. A vegetarian is someone who ___________.

    a. worships animals

    b. does not allow violence

    c. doesn't eat meat

9. Asoka became famous for _____________.

    a. his just, merciful rule

    b. the thousands of people he killed

    c. the trees he planted

    d. his strict, harsh commands

10. According to legend, the Jataka Tales were told by _____________ to show people how to live.

    a. Asoka

    b. Sakka

    c. Buddha

    d. Jackal

11. In the story we read from the Jataka Tales, who was rewarded for his generosity?

    a. the monkey

    b. the hare

    c. the otter

    d. the jackal

12. Why were the other animals not rewarded?

    a. They would not share any food.

    b. They stole their food.

    c. They did not find any food.

    d. They only ate grass.

C. True or False. Write the word "true" or "false."

__________ 13. It was very unusual for ancient cities to be united together.

__________ 14. Asoka planted trees along the road so that travelers could walk in the shade.

__________ 15. Asoka built hospitals for sick people and sick animals.

__________ 16. King Asoka gave up eating meat because of the teachings of Sakka.

Name ____ Date ____________

The Story of the World, Vol. 1

Chapter 30 Test: The People of the Americas

A. Fill in the blanks.

1. To get to the Americas from the Fertile Crescent, you have to cross the ____________ Ocean.
2. The narrow strip of land that connects North and South America is called ____.
3. South America has flat, fertile land in the middle and ________________________ all along one edge.
4. The people of the Americas did not leave ___________________________________ behind so we don't know as much about them as we know about other ancient people.

B. Multiple Choice. Circle the letter of the best choice.

5. The __________ were a tribe of people who lived along the rivers of South America in a place that is now called Peru.
   a. Nazca
   b. Meso
   c. Olmecs
   d. Macedonians
6. These people made drawings on the ground that were ____________.
   a. washed away by heavy rains
   b. carved in stone
   c. very small and hard to see
   d. hundreds of feet across
7. Some of these drawings were pictures of ______________.
   a. their great tribal leaders
   b. horses, cows, and pigs
   c. spiders, hummingbirds, and flowers
   d. huge buildings and temples

8. Archeologists think these drawings may have been made using ___________.
    a. roads and highways
    b. airplanes
    c. the sun
    d. mathematics

9. What was the name of the first civilization in Central America?
    a. Nazca
    b. Meso
    c. Olmecs
    d. Macedonians

10. Where did the rich people of this tribe live?
    a. on top of a huge pyramid of dirt and clay
    b. at the foot of the hill, on the plain
    c. in a city on a hill
    d. by the river

11. Archaeologists found huge ___________ that once surrounded these people's temple.
    a. animals
    b. heads
    c. bodies
    d. pyramids

12. The people who lived in North America left us ___________ that tell us about them.
    a. written records
    b. stories
    c. artifacts
    d. books

C. True or False. Write the word "true" or "false."

__________ 13. The ancient people of South America learned how to dry cassava roots, grind them up, and make them into banana pudding.

__________ 14. Mesoamerica means "between the Americas."

__________ 15. In the northern part of North America, the people ate corn, wheat, fish and buffalo.

__________ 16. The ancient people of North America were nomads.

Name ____ Date ______________

The Story of the World, Vol. 1

Chapter 31 Test: The Roman Republic

A. Matching. Match each god or goddess with the correct description.

____	1. Jupiter	a.	the Roman god of the sea
____	2. Mars	b.	the king of the Roman gods
____	3. Neptune	c.	the daughter of the goddess of the harvest
____	4. Ceres	d.	the king of the underworld
____	5. Proserpine	e.	the goddess of the harvest
____	6. Pluto	f.	the Roman god of war

B. Multiple Choice. Circle the letter of the best choice.

7. The Appian Way was a famous Roman _______________.

   a. bath

   b. apartment building

   c. aqueduct

   d. road

8. The Romans built _______________ to bring fresh water into the cities.

   a. baths

   b. gladiators

   c. aqueducts

   d. roads

9. Which of the following did the Romans not build?

   a. roads

   b. apartment buildings

   c. castles

   d. baths

10. How did the Romans travel from one end of the Italian peninsula to the other?

    a. They built aqueducts.
    b. They built roads.
    c. They used ships.
    d. They did not travel much.

11. The Romans took the ___________ gods as their own but gave them Roman names.

    a. Greek
    b. Babylonian
    c. Egyptian
    d. Assyrian

12. _______________ were men trained to fight with each other and with wild animals.

    a. gladiators
    b. consuls
    c. patricians
    d. aqueducts

C. True or False. Write the word "true" or "false."

__________ 13. The Romans were the first ancient people to use concrete.

__________ 14. The Roman roads were much better than most roads of the ancient world.

__________ 15. All Roman apartment buildings were well built and luxurious.

__________ 16. Today, many things built by the Romans can still be found.

__________ 17. According to the Romans, winter comes because Ceres has to spend six months of every year in the underworld.

Name ______________________________________ Date ____________

The Story of the World, Vol. 1

Chapter 32 Test: Rome's War with Carthage

A. Fill in the blanks.

1. Rome and Carthage fought for many years in the _______________________.
2. At first, Carthage had the advantage because they had a _________________________, soldiers who knew how to sail ships.
3. ______________________ was a famous general from Carthage.
4. ______________________ was the man who finally defeated him.

B. Multiple Choice. Circle the letter of the best choice.

5. Why did Rome and Carthage fight for so many years?
    a. They both wanted to control trade around the Mediterranean Sea.
    b. Rome wanted to take over all of the Carthaginian land.
    c. Carthage wanted to take over all of the Roman land.
    d. They both wanted to rule India.
6. How did the Romans learn how to build ships like the Carthaginians?
    a. They captured some Carthaginian soldiers.
    b. The Romans sent spies to Carthage.
    c. A Carthaginian sailor betrayed his country and moved to Rome.
    d. They took apart a Carthaginian ship that wrecked on the coast of Italy.
7. A Roman general named Claudius Pulcher took sacred ______________ on his ship to bring him good fortune in battle.
    a. elephants
    b. cows
    c. chickens
    d. peacocks

8. What unusual thing did the Carthaginians use to attack the Romans?

    a. elephants

    b. cannons

    c. ships

9. How did the Carthaginians sneak into Italy?

    a. They came over the mountains.

    b. They came at night.

    c. They sailed on ships.

    d. They came through Greece.

10. How did the Roman general get the Carthaginians to leave Italy?

    a. He pretended to surrender.

    b. He drove them out with his strong army.

    c. He attacked the city of Carthage.

    d. He surrounded their camp and starved them.

11. Who finally won these wars?

    a. Carthage

    b. Rome

    c. Gaul

    d. Greece

C. True or False. Write the word "true" or "false."

__________ 12. After the Romans took over all of Italy, they were content and peaceful.

__________ 13. The wars between Rome and Carthage took place entirely on land.

__________ 14. The Romans made many sacrifices to their gods asking for help in defeating Carthage.

__________ 15. When the great general of Carthage heard that the war was over, he killed himself by drinking poison.

Name ____ Date ______________

The Story of the World, Vol. 1

Chapter 33 Test: The First Dynasties of China

A. Fill in the blanks.

1. China was filled with different kingdoms ruled by warlords. We call this time "The Period of the ________________________________."
2. The ruler of the kingdom of __________________________ had an army with over a million men in it and conquered all of the other kingdoms to become the first emperor of all China.
3. Today we call the paths that travelers took from Europe, past the Mediterranan, into China, the

   "____________________________________."
4. The ________________________ Dynasty ruled for nearly 400 years and turned China into one of the richest countries in the world.

B. Multiple Choice. Circle the letter of the best choice.

5. What did Qin Zheng do to keep control of his new kingdom?
   a. He made all of the former rulers move to his capital city so he could keep an eye on them.
   b. He killed anyone who tried to rebel against him
   c. He burned thousands of books.
   d. All of the above
6. What did the people think about Qin Zheng?
   a. They loved him.
   b. They despised him for his cruelty.
   c. They thought he was fair and just.
   d. They worshipped him as a god.
7. Why did Qin Zheng build the Great Wall of China?
   a. He didn't want any of his people to escape.
   b. He wanted to keep the Mongols out of China.
   c. He was worried about the Mauryan Empire in India.
   d. He wanted to be remembered forever.

8. What did European merchants travel to China to buy?
    a. silk
    b. perfumes
    c. gold
    d. All of the above

9. What is the Great Wall of China made of?
    a. carved blocks of stone
    b. sun-baked clay
    c. rocks from the river beds
    d. stone and packed dirt

C. True or False. Write the word "true" or "false."

__________ 10. Qin Zheng changed his name to Shi Huangdi meaning "First Emperor."

__________ 11. It took fifty years to build the Great Wall of China.

__________ 12. The Great Wall of China is almost as long as the United States is wide.

__________ 13. Archaeologists found thousands of life-sized clay horses and soldiers around Qin Zheng's tomb.

__________ 14. The Silk Road is actually a network of many paths, roads, and sea passages that connect China to Europe.

Name ______________________________ Date __________

The Story of the World, Vol. 1

Chapter 34 Test: The Rise of Julius Caesar

A. Fill in the blanks.

1. Julius Caesar was born in ____________________.
2. His family claimed to be descended from ____________________, the founder of Rome.
3. His uncle was a ____________________, one of Rome's two rulers.
4. At one time, Caesar's job was governing the Roman province of ____________________.
5. Julius Caesar wanted to conquer a country called ____________________.
6. The people who lived in this country were the ____________________.

B. Multiple Choice. Circle the letter of the best choice.

7. What is rhetoric?
   a. public speaking
   b. reading
   c. writing
   d. mathematics
8. What happened when Caesar sailed out to an island in the Mediterranean Sea to take more rhetoric lessons?
   a. He was shipwrecked.
   b. His ship became lost.
   c. He became ill and almost died.
   d. He was captured by pirates.
9. What event caused everyone in Rome to know who Caesar was?
   a. He won a rhetoric competition.
   b. He won a great victory in Gaul.
   c. He captured pirates and had them executed.
   d. He was elected to the Senate.

10. Why could Caesar not become consul when he wanted to?
    a. He was not old enough.
    b. He could not get elected.
    c. He was out of the country.
    d. There were already two consuls.

11. Caesar wept when he read the story of Alexander the Great because ______________.
    a. Caesar had not yet done anything to make himself famous
    b. he was sad that Alexander died so young
    c. he wanted a great horse like Bucephalus
    d. he had never been to Greece and really wanted to go

12. The Senate worried that Caesar wanted to be ______________.
    a. the most powerful Senator
    b. the king of Rome
    c. the ruler of Egypt
    d. the ruler of Spain

13. The Senators wished that Caesar were more like ______________.
    a. Alexander the Great
    b. Cincinnatus
    c. Romulus
    d. Scipio

14. Caesar's soldiers were loyal to him because ______________.
    a. he treated them so well
    b. he paid them well
    c. he made sure they had plenty to eat
    d. All of the above

C. True or False. Write the word "true" or "false."

__________ 15. Caesar's father once said that his son would "become one of the most famous men in Rome!"

__________ 16. Caesar became popular by throwing large parties for the people he needed to vote for him.

__________ 17. Caesar was excited about his job of governing one of Rome's colonies.

__________ 18. When Caesar sent back reports to the Roman people about the wars he was fighting, he was always honest about the times when he was defeated.

Name ______________________________ Date ____________

The Story of the World, Vol. 1

Chapter 35 Test: Caesar, Ruler of Rome

A. Fill in the blanks.

1. The ____________________ convinced Pompey to turn against Caesar.
2. Caesar went to ____________________ to look for Pompey.
3. While he was there, Caesar fell in love with ____________________.
4. The month of ____________________ was named after Octavian.
5. The month of ____________________ was named after Julius Caesar.

B. Multiple Choice. Circle the letter of the best choice.

6. Why was it hard to convince Pompey to turn against Caesar?
    a. Pompey was jealous of Caesar.
    b. Pompey had married Caesar's daughter.
    c. Pompey knew that Caesar was more popular with the people than he was.
    d. Pompey thought that Caesar was a great hero.
7. What message did Pompey send to Caesar?
    a. Caesar would be arrested when he returned to Rome.
    b. Pompey would give up his job as consul.
    c. Caesar would be made king when he returned to Rome.
    d. Caesar would be killed when he returned to Rome.
8. Caesar had to cross the ____________________ River to return to Rome.
    a. Rubicon
    b. Tiber
    c. Euphrates
    d. Ganges
9. Why was it hard for Pompey to find soldiers to fight for him?
    a. No one liked Pompey.
    b. Pompey did not have enough money to pay them.
    c. All of the men who were the right age already belonged to Caesar's army.
    d. No one wanted to fight against Caesar's army.

10. What did Cleopatra's brother do to try to make friends with Caesar?
    a. He gave Caesar many gifts of gold and jewels.
    b. He sent Pompey to Caesar as a prisoner.
    c. He sent Pompey's head to Caesar in a bag.
    d. He gave Caesar part of Egypt.

11. When Julius Caesar died, Octavian ___________.
    a. threw a huge party that lasted for ten days
    b. hid in Egypt
    c. became the new king
    d. refused to see anyone

12. Octavian went to the Senate and demanded that ___________.
    a. Caesar be honored with a special statue
    b. Caesar's murderers be put to death
    c. he be made the new emperor
    d. he be made a consul

13. The Senate did not want Octavian to become a leader of Rome because ___________.
    a. he was too old
    b. the people did not like him
    c. he was too much like Caesar
    d. he did not have enough money

C. True or False. Write the word "true" or "false."

__________ 14. Caesar wanted his adopted son, Octavian, to inherit his power.

__________ 15. Many of Caesar's friends turned against him, but Brutus remained loyal.

__________ 16. Octavian's new name meant "blessed" and "majestic."

Name ______________________________ Date ____________

The Story of the World, Vol. 1

Chapter 36 Test: Israel Under Roman Rule

A. Fill in the blanks.

1. The Romans installed a "client king" over the Jews. His name was ____________________.
2. The time of peace and safety in the Roman Empire was called the ____________________ ____________________.
3. We can read about Jesus in the four books of the Bible called the ____________________.
4. Many people celebrate the birth of Jesus on ____________________.
5. The people who followed Jesus became known as ____________________.

B. Multiple Choice. Circle the letter of the best choice.

6. The Romans called Herod "the Great" because ____________.
   a. he was beloved by the Jewish people.
   b. he fought and won many battles.
   c. he constructed huge buildings.
   d. he was known to be wise and fair.

7. ____________ was the mother of Jesus.
   a. Anna
   b. Elizabeth
   c. Mary
   d. Sarah

8. When Jesus grew up, his most famous teaching was given ____________.
   a. to the chief priests
   b. in the temple
   c. to Augustus Caesar
   d. on the side of a mountain

9. The Gospel of Luke says that after Jesus died, he was put into a tomb, and after three days, ______________________.
   a. he came back to life.
   b. his followers began mourning for him.
   c. he went to heaven.
   d. he appeared to Caesar Augustus.

10. What did the Jewish fighters do when they rebelled against Rome?
    a. They set fire to the house of the Roman ruler of Judea.
    b. Armed groups of Jewish men attacked Roman soldiers.
    c. They killed the emperor.
    d. Both a and b

11. What did the emperor order the Roman soldiers to do?
    a. Destroy the whole city of Jerusalem
    b. Burn down all of Herod's buildings
    c. Chase the Jewish soldiers out of the country
    d. Make peace with the Jews

12. What happened to the Jews?
    a. They were scattered throughout all the countries of the ancient world.
    b. They remained in Canaan, but were never again a strong nation.
    c. They conquered the Romans.
    d. They were all killed.

C. True or False. Write the word "true" or "false."

__________ 13. Jesus was not very popular with the people of Judea.

__________ 14. The Jewish religious leaders worried that Jesus might start a rebellion against the Romans.

__________ 15. The Zealots at Masada killed themselves instead of surrendering to the Romans.

Name ______________________________ Date ____________

The Story of the World, Vol. 1

Chapter 37 Test: Rome and the Christians

A. Fill in the blanks.

1. Nero, one of the worst Roman emperors, loved ______________________________ even though he was terrible at it.
2. When Rome burned, Nero blamed the ________________________.
3. The Christians held meetings in underground passages called _____________________.
4. The Romans punished slaves, criminals, and Christians by making them fight _____________________.

B. Multiple Choice. Circle the letter of the best choice.

5. Why were people so afraid of Nero?
    a. Nero was so similar to Augustus Caesar.
    b. Nero tried to put spells on people.
    c. Nero had everyone who disagreed with him murdered.
    d. Nero stole money from a lot of people.
6. When the city of Rome burned, Nero was ____________.
    a. watching from his palace
    b. visiting Egypt
    c. in another city at a meeting
    d. in the country giving a huge party
7. What did Nero do at first, when he heard about the fire?
    a. He gave money to all of the poor families.
    b. He rebuilt all of the buildings that had been burned down.
    c. He stayed where he was for several more days.
    d. He built a new capital city.

8. The Roman emperors did not like the Christians because the Christians _____________.
    a. would not worship the emperor
    b. were becoming wealthier than the Romans
    c. disobeyed all of the Roman laws
    d. were encouraging the Roman people to rebel

9. The Christians used a _____________ as a secret symbol to identify other Christians.
    a. fish
    b. cross
    c. Greek word for Jesus
    d. dove

C. True or False. Write the word "true" or "false."

__________ 10. The Roman people were grateful to Nero for helping them after the burning of Rome.

__________ 11. The Romans worshipped the emperor as one of their gods.

__________ 12. Many Christians were forced to fight in gladiator shows or be killed by wild animals during Nero's reign.

Name ________________________________ Date ____________

The Story of the World, Vol. 1

Chapter 38 Test: Rome Begins to Weaken

A. Fill in the blanks.

1. Boadicea was the leader of a tribe of ______________ in the Roman province of Britain.
2. The Romans were embarrassed to be beaten by Boadicea because Boadicea was a ____________________.
3. ____________________ was the emperor who decided to divide the empire into two parts.
4. He ruled the ____________________ half and chose someone else to rule the other half.

B. Multiple Choice. Circle the letter of the best choice.

5. The Roman Empire began to weaken because ____________.
   - a. there were many bad emperors
   - b. some of the countries that Rome had conquered began to rebel
   - c. the empire was getting so large
   - d. All of the above
6. Why did the Romans finally win against Boadicea?
   - a. They had more men in their army.
   - b. They had better weapons.
   - c. They had better maps of the area.
   - d. They stayed together in battle and obeyed their general.
7. Why did the size of the Roman Empire cause problems?
   - a. The emperor could not visit all of the different cities to meet the people.
   - b. There were no good roads to travel from one end of the empire to another.
   - c. The borders were too long for one army to protect.
   - d. There was not enough food for such a large empire.

8. When the empire was split, who was chosen to rule the other half of the empire?

    a. Boadicea

    b. Diocletian

    c. Constantine

    d. Maximian

9. Constantine ended the persecution of the Christians because ___________ .

    a. he was a Christian too

    b. he didn't think it was right to put people in jail because of who they worshipped

    c. he wanted the Christians to think he was a good emperor

    d. the Christians paid him a lot of money

10. What did Constantine see in the sky before an important battle?

    a. a fish made out of clouds

    b. a picture of Jesus

    c. a cross of light

    d. the army of God

11. What happened to Constantine after the battle?

    a. He started persecuting the Christians again.

    b. He became a Christian.

    c. He returned to Rome.

    d. He took a trip to Jerusalem.

C. True or False. Write the word "true" or "false."

__________ 12. Julius Caesar and Augustus Caesar were two of Rome's strongest rulers.

__________ 13. The Roman settlement of Londinium became the city of London.

__________ 14. The Romans conquered Britain, but they did not stay in control for long.

__________ 15. Invaders attacked the Roman Empire in Britain, Gaul, Spain, and Italy itself.

__________ 16. If you go to Italy today, you will not see any remains of the Roman Empire.

Name ______________________________ Date ____________

The Story of the World, Vol. 1

Chapter 39 Test: Troubles in China

A. Fill in the blanks.

1. Because trade along the ________________ was so important, hundreds of young men were forced to join bands of soldiers who kept the ________________ safe from thieves and highwaymen.

2. Chang Chueh told his followers that they could not be ____________________ in battle.

3. After the Han emperor fled, the Han kingdom fractured into ____________________ pieces.

B. Multiple Choice. Circle the letter of the best choice.

4. In 184 CE, a band of warriors who called themselves the ____________ declared that they were ready to fight.

   a. Red Wave

   b. Yellow Turbans

   c. Blue Storm

   d. People's Army

5. Chang Chueh, their leader, claimed that he was a ________________.

   a. God

   b. Prince

   c. Magician

   d. Poor farmer

6. Instead of fighting the rebellion, General Dong Zhuo took his army and _____________.

   a. Marched into the capital city of Han China

   b. Captured the thirteen-year-old emperor

   c. Declared himself ruler of the Han

   d. All of the above

7. After Dong Zhuo died, Ts'ao Ts'ao ________________.

    a. Made himself the official emperor

    b. Forced the emperor to marry his daughter

    c. died from a battle wound

    d. Formed a democracy

C. True or False. Write the word "true" or "false."

__________ 8. For over fifty years, the Han had children as emperors.

__________ 9. Dong Zhuo and Ts'ao Ts'ao were both generals for the Han government.

__________ 10. Wei Yuandi gave General Sima Yan (Jin Wudi) control of China because they were friends.

__________ 11. Jin Wudi conquered the other two kingdoms and became ruler over all China.

__________ 12. After Jin Wudi died, his only son inherited the throne and maintained the power of the Jin Empire.

__________ 13. The Sixteen Kingdoms refused to adopt the customs of the Jin or speak the Jin language.

Name ______________________________ Date ____________

The Story of the World, Vol. 1

Chapter 40 Test: Lands East of China

A. Fill in the blanks.

1. In the days of the Han Empire, the Korean peninsula was divided into ____________ kingdoms.
2. The kingdom of ________________ had always been the most troublesome to the Han.
3. When King Micheon died, his son turned out to be a much ________________ ruler.
4. Japan was originally ruled by ________________, families with their own territories and their own government.

B. Multiple Choice. Circle the letter of the best choice.

5. Which of the Korean kingdoms conquered the Han cities in the north?
   a. Goguryeo
   b. Baekje
   c. Silla
   d. Jin
6. After King Micheon died, the armies of the Sixteen Kingdoms __________.
   a. signed a treaty with Goguryeo
   b. invaded Goguryeo over and over again
   c. left Goguryeo for good
   d. forced everyone to stop speaking Chinese
7. King Sosurim helped his country survive by __________.
   a. rewarding soldiers for joining his army
   b. strengthening his borders
   c. rebuilding Goguryeo's damaged cities
   d. All of the above

8. Japan is made up of ____________ big islands and over seven thousand small islands.

    a. two

    b. three

    c. four

    d. five

9. According to Yamato legend, Amaterasu was given ____________ to rule over.

    a. the entire sky

    b. the entire sea

    c. the entire world

    d. the underworld

10. Susano fled from the sky down to earth because he ____________.

    a. lost the war with Amaterasu

    b. was scared of his father

    c. had too many children

    d. was fleeing from the eight-headed serpent

C. True or False. Write the word "true" or "false."

_________ 11. The Yamato emperors said they were descendants of the Sun Goddess Amaterasu.

_________ 12. It took less than 100 years for the Yamato leaders to rule all of Japan.

Name ______________________________ Date ____________

The Story of the World, Vol. 1

Chapter 41 Test: The Attacking Barbarians

A. Fill in the blanks.

1. ________________ was a brave Roman fighter whose father was a barbarian.

2. The ________________ were a group of barbarians who destroyed the city of Rome.

3. The Huns were a group of barbarians from Central Asia who attacked Rome on strong, fast ______________________.

B. Multiple Choice. Circle the letter of the best choice.

4. How did Stilicho get the Visigoths to leave Rome?
   a. He gave them four thousand pounds of gold.
   b. He defeated them after many battles.
   c. He married the daughter of their leader.
   d. He killed their leader.

5. When the emperor heard that the Visigoths were again planning to invade Rome, he ____________.
   a. killed himself
   b. gathered together a small army to defend the city
   c. fled to a small city in the middle of a swamp
   d. sent them a letter begging them to leave

6. Why didn't the Eastern Roman Empire send help?
   a. They did not like the Western Roman Empire.
   b. The emperor was afraid that the barbarians would attack his own city.
   c. They had become allies with the Visigoths.
   d. They did send help, but it arrived too late.

7. When the Visigoths invaded the city of Rome, they ____________.
   a. ripped down golden statues and stole coins and jewelry
   b. took the people of Rome as hostages
   c. destroyed Rome's churches
   d. did not harm anything in the city

8. The leader of the Huns was ___________.

    a. Honoria

    b. Attila

    c. Alaric

    d. Stilicho

9. The Roman emperor's sister sent a letter to the leader of the Huns offering to ___________.

    a. surrender to him

    b. give him thousands of pounds of gold

    c. introduce him to her brother

    d. marry him

10. Why did the Huns leave Italy after a successful invasion?

    a. The emperor paid them a large amount of money.

    b. The emperor gave their leader his sister in marriage.

    c. The Roman army drove them back out.

    d. The did not like living in Rome.

11. What happened to the Huns' leader before he could marry the emperor's sister?

    a. A Roman soldier killed him.

    b. His own men killed him.

    c. He died of a nosebleed.

    d. Another group of barbarians captured him.

C. True or False. Write the word "true" or "false."

__________ 12. Some barbarians grew to like the Roman way of life and sometimes switched sides.

__________ 13. Many Romans felt bad after they executed Stilicho.

__________ 14. When the Eastern Roman Empire heard that Rome had been invaded, they rejoiced.

__________ 15. The Huns taught their babies to ride horseback even before they could walk.

__________ 16. The Huns built a huge monument over the grave of their great leader.

Name ______________________________________ Date _____________

The Story of the World, Vol. 1

Chapter 42 Test: The End of Rome

A. Fill in the blanks.

1. After the Roman Empire divided, the Eastern Roman Empire continued. We now call it the ______________________ Empire.

2. ____________________________________ was the last Roman emperor.

B. Multiple Choice. Circle the letter of the best choice.

3. An invader named __________________ decided to drive the Roman Emperor out of hiding.

    a. Alaric

    b. Attila

    c. Orestes

    d. Stilicho

4. When the emperor heard that he was coming he _____________.

    a. ran away

    b. surrendered to him

    c. gathered an army for one last fight

    d. sent him thousands of pounds of gold

5. The Romans called their last emperor "Momyllus" which means _____________.

    a. little ruler

    b. great ruler

    c. last

    d. little disgrace

6. What happened to the land that once belonged to Rome?

    a. It became part of the Eastern Roman empire.

    b. It was given to the Huns.

    c. It was divided among the various barbarian kings.

    d. It all became the country of France.

C. True or False. Write the word "true" or "false."

_________ 7. The Romans loved their last emperor.

_________ 8. When the people of the Eastern Roman Empire heard that the Western Roman Empire was gone, they mourned.

_________ 9. The Romans gave us many words and inventions that we use today.

D. Match each English word with the Latin word it comes from (one word will not be used).

____ 10.	refrigerator	a. scriptum
____ 11.	family	b. liber
____ 12.	library	c. floris
____ 13.	navy	d. navis
____ 14.	flower	e. familia
		f. frigidarium

E. Name three things other than words that we get from the Romans.

15. ____

16. ____

17. ____

The Story of the World
Volume 1: Ancient Times

ANSWER KEY

Chapter 1 Test

1. nomad
2. tents
3. caves
4. the Fertile Crescent
5. canals
6. b
7. c
8. d
9. a
10. c
11. b
12. b
13. true
14. false
15. true
16. false
17. false
18. true

Chapter 2 Test

1. Africa
2. flood
3. Lower Egyptians
4. Upper Egyptians
5. pharaoh
6. a
7. c
8. b
9. c
10. d
11. a
12. b
13. true
14. true
15. false
16. true
17. false
18. true

Chapter 3 Test

1. Egyptians
2. hieroglyphics
3. Sumer
4. cuneiform
5. a
6. c
7. b
8. d
9. a
10. c
11. false
12. false
13. true
14. true
15. true

Chapter 4 Test

1. mummies
2. priests
3. heart
4. three
5. pyramids
6. b
7. a
8. d
9. b
10. a
11. b
12. true
13. true
14. true
15. false
16. false

Chapter 5 Test

1. Mesopotamia
2. Sumerians
3. city-states
4. Sargon
5. Kish
6. d
7. b
8. a
9. c
10. c
11. true
12. true
13. false
14. true
15. true

Chapter 6 Test

1. Ur
2. Genesis
3. Canaan
4. twelve
5. Egypt
6. a
7. c
8. d
9. a
10. b
11. d
12. c
13. true
14. false
15. true
16. true
17. false
18. false

Chapter 7 Test

1. Babylonia
2. The Code of Hammurabi
3. one year
4. twelve
5. a
6. c
7. d
8. a
9. b
10. true
11. false
12. true
13. true
14. false

Chapter 8 Test

1. northern	2. Assyrian	3. Gilgamesh	4. snake	5. b
6. b	7. a	8. d	9. c	10. a
11. true	12. true	13. false	14. true	15. false

Chapter 9 Test

1. trading	2. rivers	3. Indus	4. citadels	5. c
6. c	7. a	8. b	9. d	10. a
11. false	12. true	13. true	14. false	15. true

Chapter 10 Test

1. Yellow	2. rice	3. silk	4. dynasty	5. pictograms
6. b	7. c	8. b	9. a	10. d
11. d	12. a	13. true	14. true	15. true
16. false	17. false			

Chapter 11 Test

1. Sahara Desert	2. oases	3. water	4. Anansi the Spider	5. a
6. d	7. a	8. b	9. b	10. d
11. true	12. true	13. true	14. false	15. true

Chapter 12 Test

1. Minoans	2. Mediterranean	3. bulls	4. navy	5. Minotaur
6. b	7. c	8. b	9. a	10. d
11. c	12. a	13. c	14. false	15. true
16. true	17. false	18. true		

Chapter 13 Test

1. Nubia	2. Kush	3. dynasty	4. Canaan	5. c
6. a	7. d	8. a	9. b	10. b
11. c	12. false	13. true	14. false	15. false
16. true				

Chapter 14 Test

1. b	2. d	3. a	4. c	5. true
6. false	7. false	8. false	9. true	10. d
11. a	12. a	13. c	14. b	15. b
16. d	17. c			

Chapter 15 Test

1. Abraham	2. slaves	3. Moses	4. Red Sea	5. Exodus
6. a	7. d	8. c	9. c	10. a
11. b	12. d	13. true	14. false	15. false
16. false	17. true	18. true		

Chapter 16 Test

1. c	2. b	3. a	4. d	5. a
6. a	7. c	8. b	9. c	10. d
11. b	12. a	13. true	14. true	15. false
16. false				

Chapter 17 Test

1. Canaan	2. Mediterranean Sea	3. Carthage and Tyre	4. glass and purple dye	5. d
6. b	7. c	8. c	9. a	10. c
11. false	12. true	13. true	14. false	15. true

Chapter 18 Test

1. baskets	2. cruel	3. Nineveh	4. librarian	5. c
6. b	7. a	8. a	9. d	10. c
11. true	12. true	13. false	14. true	15. false

Chapter 19 Test

1. d	2. c	3. a	4. b	5. c
6. a	7. a	8. b	9. d	10. b
11. a	12. c	13. true	14. true	15. false
16. true	17. false	18. false		

Chapter 20 Test

1. Athens	2. Sparta	3. agora	4. democracy	5. b
6. c	7. a	8. d	9. a	10. b
11. b	12. d	13. d	14. false	15. false
16. true	17. true	18. false		

Chapter 21 Test

1. b	2. f	3. e	4. h	5. d
6. c	7. a	8. g	9. c	10. a
11. d	12. d	13. b	14. c	15. a
16. true	17. false	18. true		

Chapter 22 Test

1. seven	2. Italy	3. Etruscans	4. togas	5. b
6. a	7. c	8. d	9. d	10. a
11. b	12. d	13. true	14. true	15. false

Chapter 23 Test

1. animal	2. Daniel	3. Media	4. Hanging Gardens	5. a
6. c	7. b	8. a	9. d	10. b
11. c	12. false	13. true	14. false	15. false
16. true				

Chapter 24 Test

1. Medes	2. shepherds	3. Cyrus	4. Greece	5. a
6. d	7. c	8. d	9. a	10. c
11. b	12. b	13. true	14. false	15. true
16. true	17. false	18. true		

Chapter 25 Test

1. Asia	2. Ganges	3. Hinduism	4. caste	5. a
6. b	7. d	8. c	9. a	10. d
11. b	12. c	13. true	14. false	15. true
16. true	17. false			

Chapter 26 Test

1. calligraphy	2. character	3. animal hairs	4. printing	5. b
6. c	7. a	8. a	9. a	10. d
11. true	12. false	13. false	14. true	

Chapter 27 Test

1. Athens	2. Persia	3. Parthenon	4. Sparta	5. a
6. d	7. c	8. b	9. a	10. c
11. b	12. b	13. true	14. false	15. false
16. true	17. true			

Chapter 28 Test

1. Macedonia	2. Persian	3. lighthouse	4. Alexandria	5. c
6. c	7. a	8. d	9. b	10. d
11. c	12. false	13. true	14. true	15. true
16. false				

Chapter 29 Test

1. united	2. Asoka	3. Buddha	4. Jataka Tales	5. a
6. d	7. c	8. c	9. a	10. c
11. b	12. b	13. false	14. true	15. true
16. false				

Chapter 30 Test

1. Atlantic	2. Central America	3. mountains	4. written records	5. a
6. d	7. c	8. d	9. c	10. c
11. b	12. b	13. false	14. true	15. false
16. true				

Chapter 31 Test

1. b	2. f	3. a	4. e	5. c
6. d	7. d	8. c	9. c	10. b
11. a	12. a	13. true	14. true	15. false
16. true	17. false			

Chapter 32 Test

1. Punic Wars
2. navy
3. Hannibal
4. Scipio
5. a
6. d
7. c
8. a
9. a
10. c
11. b
12. false
13. false
14. true
15. true

Chapter 33 Test

1. Warring States
2. Qin
3. Silk Road
4. Han
5. d
6. b
7. b
8. d
9. d
10. true
11. false
12. true
13. true
14. true

Chapter 34 Test

1. Rome
2. Romulus
3. consul
4. Spain
5. Britain
6. Celts
7. a
8. d
9. c
10. d
11. a
12. b
13. b
14. d
15. true
16. true
17. false
18. false

Chapter 35 Test

1. senators
2. Egypt
3. Cleopatra
4. August
5. July
6. b
7. a
8. a
9. d
10. c
11. a
12. d
13. c
14. true
15. false
16. true

Chapter 36 Test

1. Herod
2. Pax Romana
3. Gospels
4. Christmas
5. Christians
6. c
7. c
8. d
9. a
10. d
11. a
12. a
13. false
14. true
15. true

Chapter 37 Test

1. music
2. Christians
3. catacombs
4. wild animals
5. c
6. d
7. c
8. a
9. a
10. false
11. true
12. true

Chapter 38 Test

1. Celts
2. woman
3. Diocletian
4. eastern
5. d
6. d
7. c
8. d
9. b
10. c
11. b
12. true
13. true
14. true
15. true
16. false

Chapter 39 Test

1. Silk Road...Silk Road
2. wounded
3. three
4. b
5. c
6. d
7. b
8. true
9. true
10. false
11. true
12. false
13. false

Chapter 40 Test

1. three	2. Goguryeo	3. weaker	4. clans	5. a
6. b	7. d	8. c	9. a	10. a
11. true	12. false			

Chapter 41 Test

1. Stilicho	2. Vandals	3. warhorses	4. a	5. c
6. b	7. a	8. b	9. d	10. a
11. c	12. true	13. true	14. false	15. true
16. false				

Chapter 42 Test

1. Byzantine	2. Romulus Augustus	3. c	4. a	5. d
6. c	7. false	8. true	9. true	10. f
11. e	12. b	13. d	14. c	

15–17. answers will vary